D1729577

THE PSYCHIC ARTS

TAROT

BY MEGAN ATWOOD

Consultant: Lisa Raggio-Kimmins, M.A., Psychology and Counseling

COMPASS POINT BOOKS
a capstone imprint

Psychic Arts is published by Compass Point Books, a Capstone imprint
1710 Roe Crest Drive, North Mankato, Minnesota, 56003.
www.mycapstone.com

Copyright © 2019 by Capstone Press, a Capstone imprint. All rights reserved. No part of this publication may be reproduced in whole or in part, or stored in a retrieval system, or transmitted in any form or by any means, electronic, mechanical, photocopying, recording, or otherwise, without written permission of the publisher.

Library of Congress Cataloging-in-Publication Data
ISBN 978-0-7565-6101-7 (library binding)
ISBN 978-0-7565-6106-2 (ebook PDF)

Editorial Credits
Michelle Bisson, editor
Rachel Tesch, designer/illustrator
Svetlana Zhurkin, media researcher
Kathy McColley, production specialist

Photo Credits
Alamy: Charles Walker Collection, 9 (bottom right), 11 (bottom), Walter Oleksy, 9 (top); Capstone Studio: Karon Dubke, 12, 26, 27, 28, 29, 32, 33, 34, 35, 40; Dreamstime: Ionutadventures, 4; Getty Images: DeAgostini, 8; iStockphoto: duncan1890, 10 (right); Newscom: akg-images, 10 (left), Heritage Images/Fine Art Images, 11 (top); Shutterstock: AjayTvm, 7, bigjom jom, 9 (bottom left), bjphotographs, 42, Carlos Andre Santos, 23, JohnRex, 45 (bottom), Lena Pan, 45 (top), Mike Ver Sprill, 36, Morakot Kawinchan, 24, n_defender, 6, Photology1971, 16, Quality Stock Arts, cover

Illustrations from the Rider-Waite Tarot Deck® reproduced by permission of U.S. Games Systems, Inc., Stamford, CT 06902 USA. Copyright ©1971 by U.S. Games Systems, Inc. Further reproduction prohibited. The Rider-Waite Tarot Deck® is a registered trademark of U.S. Games Systems, Inc.

Printed and bound in the United States of America
PA49

TABLE OF CONTENTS

CHAPTER 1
It's in the Cards: Introduction to the Tarot 5

CHAPTER 2
Tarot Through the Ages: The History
and Science of Tarot 9

CHAPTER 3
How to Read: Spreads to Use 13

CHAPTER 4
What the Cards Mean: Digging
into the Major Arcana 25

CHAPTER 5
What the Cards Mean, Part 2: Digging
into the Minor Arcana 37

CHAPTER 6
Make It your own! 43

    Tarot Glossary 47

    Additional Resources 47

    Index 48

CHAPTER 1

IT'S IN THE CARDS: INTRODUCTION TO THE TAROT

You've seen the cards in movies. It starts like this: The camera stays on a woman, usually draped in scarves, wearing big hoop earrings. She has a crystal ball near her and she's turning over cards slowly from an extra-large, ancient-looking deck. But they're not playing cards—they have pictures on them. Frightening pictures of death, devils, and misfortune. The woman widens her eyes, and maybe a gust of wind breezes through the place, blowing out candles. The cards have spoken—SOMETHING BAD.

While reading tarot cards can bring up some big feelings, rarely will it be that dramatic. The cards have been used to signify something mystical in all sorts of popular culture—for good reason. Tarot cards and the images on them tap into our inner voice or intuition. Using the cards to connect and reflect on ourselves and others, as well as our past, present, and future situations, has been a helpful tool for people for generations. This book is a great first step in discovering all that tarot has to offer.

FORTUNE-TELLING VS. INNER GUIDANCE

TAROT TELLS YOU YOUR FUTURE, RIGHT?

You might be reading this book because you want to know what your life has in store for you. And, yes, tarot can be used to get a feel for the future. But many believe that the tarot works best when you use the cards as a window into what energies you or the person whose cards you're reading are dealing with. Or, to use them as a way for you to "speak" with your higher self. Maybe you want to know how to feel stronger in your everyday life. Maybe you want to see what your reactions are when you draw a daily card and meditate on it through your whole day. Though you can use the tarot as a fortune-telling tool, it is also a fantastic way to get to know yourself better and to look for ways to deepen your experience in the world right now.

HOW TO READ THIS BOOK

A tarot deck has 78 cards in all. Fifty-six of them—the Minor Arcana—echo normal playing cards with their suits and their court (meaning, royalty) cards. The other cards are the Major Arcana, which consist of 22 numbered cards (starting at 0) that are of bigger significance in a reading. This book will just touch on the meanings of the Major Arcana and even more briefly on the Minor Arcana. We'll discuss setting up a reading first, and then we'll talk about the meanings of the cards. Keep in mind that this book is just the tip of the iceberg for what is out there for tarot. Make sure to check out the additional resources in the back of the book!

FINDING YOUR DECK

To read tarot, of course you need a deck! The Rider-Waite Tarot deck is considered the "standard" deck in tarot—however, that doesn't mean it's the only one to use! Many stores sell tarot decks. Ask if you can look at the deck, or check them out online to find the one that speaks to you. Bring your parent or guardian to the store, or have them check out the decks with you online to find one that's just right for you.

Italian nobles playing with tarot cards in the mid-1400s

CHAPTER 2

TAROT THROUGH THE AGES: THE HISTORY AND SCIENCE OF TAROT

The Rider-Waite tarot deck has been around since 1909. Artist Pamela Colman Smith collaborated with A.E. Waite and William Rider to develop the deck that has become the standard in tarot. But tarot has been around for much, much longer than the 20th century.

Rider-Waite Deck (left); A.E. White 1909 booklet (right)

Some historians believe the cards originated in 14th century Europe, where a series of cards with four different suits was used to play games. In 15th century northern Italy, the game and cards became popular. Wealthy people commissioned more cards to be added, called "triumph cards." These were shortened to "trump cards" and are now known as the Major Arcana. People used them to play a game called "tarocchi appropriati." The duke of Milan, Franceso Visconti, was said to have commissioned a deck in 1415.

Napoleon Bonaparte looking at the mummy of a pharoah in Egypt

a couple playing a card game in the late 1400s

Though the tarot originally started as a game, different artists delved into the Major Arcana cards and added more symbolism and depth. The cards show a journey through life that is full of light and dark. Over time, people began to see deeper meanings in the cards. More and more, the deck's Major Arcana cards were used for divination and insight.

It wasn't until the 18th century, though, that the tarot became more widely used in this way. French emperor Napoleon Bonaparte had invaded Egypt, and artifacts from Egyptian tombs and Egyptian esoteric systems began to spread to the West.

Spurring this popularity was Antoine Court de Gébelin in France, who merged Egyptian mysticism with the tarot. He positioned the tarot as a form of esoteric knowledge formerly only held by clergy and mystics. People loved the idea that they could use such a formerly exclusive system themselves, and the tarot's popularity grew.

Jean-Baptiste Alliette, known as Etteilla, popularized the first tarot deck that was used specifically for divination and not as a game.

Fast-forward a couple of hundred years. Many mystic systems today connect with the tarot—systems such as astrology and numerology. Used with other systems, or as a method that stands alone, the tarot is still going strong. The versatility of the tarot means it speaks to people in all sorts of traditions—it transcends any one system of belief and is used as a universal language. Nowadays you can find a deck that suits you particularly and fits your style. The Rider-Waite deck maintains its popularity because each card is rich in symbols. From the colors in the illustrations to the postures to what's included in the scene, there's a lot to connect to in every single card. Other tarot decks, though, use their own style and illustrations to impart the same sorts of symbolism. The important part about the tarot deck is how you feel about it.

THE TAROT IS A WAY TO CONNECT WITH OTHER PEOPLE

Tarot is a tool that is both personal and universal, and at its very core, it is a way to connect to your higher self and to other people. Its deep history and mystic associations give you a richness and depth to explore your world and your relationships and to make the best use of your life.

two French tarot cards from the late 1700s

CHAPTER 3

HOW TO READ: SPREADS TO USE

Reading tarot cards for yourself and others can be a lot of fun—and very fulfilling. To get to know the cards really well, take out one card every day and read all about it. Check in this book for its meaning. Do some digging on the Internet. See what the majority of sites and books say the card means. Most importantly: Check what it means for you! That is, look at the illustrations and think about what you see. What is speaking to you? What is the feel of the card—does it feel ominous? Happy? Melancholic? Write down these thoughts and feelings to really explore the cards. How you read them is just as important as what others think!

When reading for others,

YOU'LL FIND THAT PEOPLE SHARE A LOT WITH YOU

once you start interpreting the cards.

KEY INTO THAT WHEN DOING READINGS!

You'll find yourself being a shoulder to cry on and a confidante.

THE TAROT DIGS DEEP INTO OUR PSYCHES.

Be aware that you're diving into deep waters and treat yourself, others, and the tarot with respect.

No matter what, when reading, remember that

YOU ARE THE AUTHOR OF YOUR OWN LIFE.

TAROT IS A TOOL FOR YOU AND THE PEOPLE YOU READ TO USE.

IT'S NOT A SET DESTINY.

YOU make the choices that craft your life.

 get to chart your course.

TAROT CAN HELP WITH THAT.

MAKE SURE TO USE IT THAT WAY! YOU'RE IN CONTROL!

How you lay out your cards and in what order is important. These are called "spreads"—you lay your cards out into a particular spread where each position has meaning.

Before starting your reading, shuffle the cards well. Think about what question you or the person you're reading for has. Also think about the spread you're going to use. If you are reading for another person, have them shuffle the cards too, and think about their question. Once this is all done, you're ready to start the reading and to put the cards into a spread. This section will go into some of the more traditional spreads, then into some spreads for your age group, and then end with exploring how you can make your own spreads!

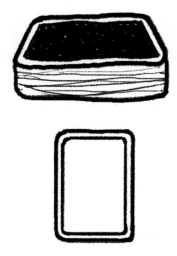

ONE-CARD SPREAD

The easiest and most common spread is the one-card spread. You can use this to ask a quick question to which you want a clear answer. Some ask a yes or no question and flip the top card over: If it's upright—that is, the picture is oriented the right way—the answer is yes; if the picture is upside down (called reversed) the answer is no. Another way to read it is to flip over a card and see what the meaning of the card is. If it's a typically happy meaning, the answer is yes. So, for example, if you ask, "Will Jamie go to the dance with me?" and the answer is the Sun, chances are you're going with Jamie!

THREE-CARD SPREAD

The three-card spread is often used too. The most common meaning of this spread is that the cards indicate the past, present, and future of a situation. But you don't necessarily have to use them that way. Maybe you want to figure out the beginning, middle, and end of a situation. Maybe you want to understand the mind, body, and heart of something. Or you might want to look at different facets of your life: school, family, and relationships. The three-card spread is a great way to ask about different sides of many different situations.

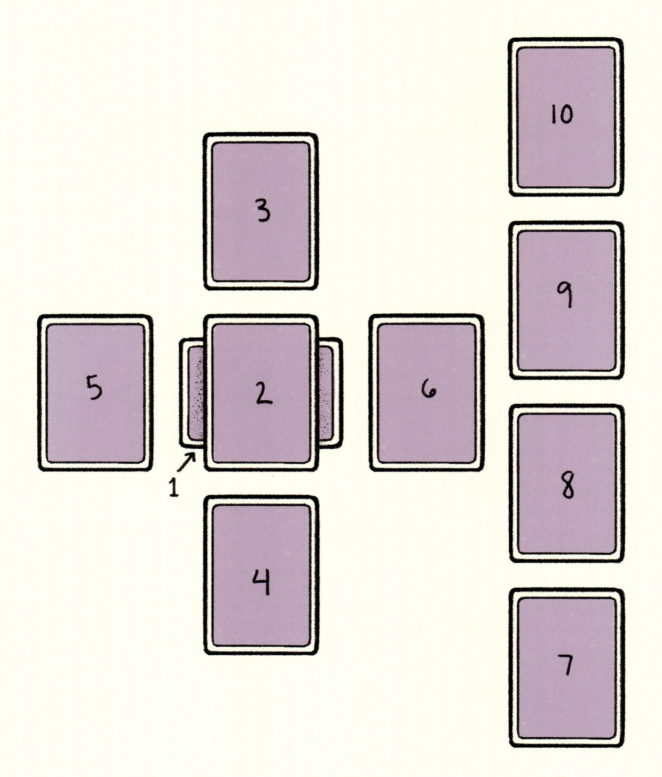

CELTIC CROSS SPREAD

The Celtic Cross is the most-used spread. You have probably seen it in movies—it looks like a cross and then four cards in a vertical line to the right of it. The Celtic Cross is a useful and dynamic tool that looks at the whole of whatever question you're asking. Here is the positioning and order of the cards, and what the positions mean.

Keep in mind that different people read the cards differently, and this interpretation is only one way of reading them!

1. This card is you in the question.

2. These are the obstacles you face, or, if positive, what tools you have to face the situation.

3. This is the deep past—the foundation of your question or why you're asking it.

4. This card represents the most recent past events.

5. In this card, you can see your possible future way out.

6. This card is the immediate future, or what is probably going to happen soon.

7. This card is how you see yourself in the situation.

8. In this card, you see how others see you in the situation, or the environment surrounding you at this time.

9. This shows your hopes and fears about the situation.

10. This is the final outcome of your question, or what to expect if everything stays the same around the situation.

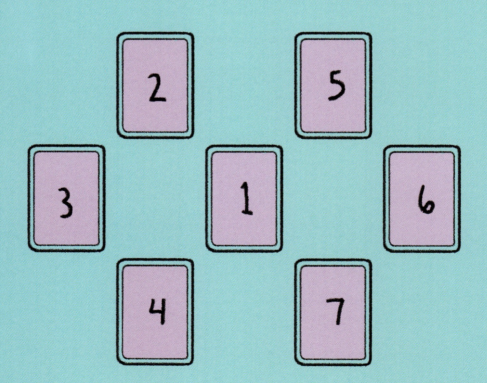

The following spreads are ones that may be right up your alley at this time in your life. The spreads will show the order the cards should be drawn, and what the positions mean.

FRIEND SPREAD

If you have a question about a specific friendship, this spread will do the trick.

1. You.

2. Your friend.

3. The strengths in your friendship.

4. The challenges in your friendship.

5. What your friendship is based on.

6. What is the next best move for your friendship?

SCHOOL SPREAD

For a general reading about the state of your school experience, try this one.

1. You.

2-4. Your schoolwork. If you have specific questions about classes, you could have the card positions indicate something specific.

5-7. Your extracurricular activities. Again, if you have specific questions about certain activities, make the positions mean something specific.

READING REVERSALS

EACH BOOKLET THAT COMES WITH A DECK HAS A "REVERSED" MEANING FOR EACH CARD. THAT REFERS TO A CARD THAT IS UPSIDE DOWN IN A READING. THERE ARE MANY WAYS TO READ REVERSED CARDS, BUT THE MOST IMPORTANT WAY IS FOR YOU TO CHOOSE A WAY AND STICK WITH IT! HERE ARE SOME WAYS TO READ REVERSALS:

Don't. Many tarot readers won't read reversals at all. Each tarot card has a few different meanings—some good, some bad. To some, reversals aren't necessary and just muddy up a reading. You might want to ignore them too as you are learning to do readings. It's a little hard to remember the meanings of 78 cards, let alone what each of them means upside down!

Some read reversals the same as upright—just less so. So if you get the Star card, you would read it as its normal meaning: The Star card means hope and optimism, and light in the darkness. But, if it's reversed, you would say this energy is weakened. So it's the same meaning as the upright card, just not quite as intense.

Other people read reversals as the opposite of what the upright meaning is. So that same Star card would read as hope lost, and as darkness swallowing up light.

You could read reversals as a blockage of the energy of the card. That is, whatever the card means, you're having a hard time with it. So again, using the Star card, you would say that hope is being blocked in the person getting the reading. Not that hope isn't there—just that that energy is blocked by something else.

Whatever you choose to do, close your eyes, hold your deck, and "tell" it how you are going to read the reversals. You might feel a little goofy doing it—understandably! But it's a good way to set the intention for yourself and to fill your cards with the energy you want to impart.

MAKING YOUR OWN SPREADS

No matter what spread you use, the energy and interpretation comes from you—so why not make your own spreads? After you've done some readings, you'll get to know how you best like to read. Then, you can figure out what configuration will best work for the questions and person you're reading for. Consider how many cards you want the spread to be. Think of what the positions of the cards will be and what each position means. You could even get a notebook and keep track of the different spreads you try to see which work the best for you in different situations. Make this your own!

CHAPTER 4

WHAT THE CARDS MEAN: DIGGING INTO THE MAJOR ARCANA

You have the tarot deck that speaks to you and you've been working on the spreads you want to use. Now comes the fun part: the card meanings! The best part of the cards is that the interpretation is subjective. That means that there may be some "typical" meanings of cards, but you get to put your own spin on them.

When you're looking at your cards, take note of what you feel when you look at each one. When you see the Magician—a card about someone in control of the elements—do you get a feeling of mastery or magic? Or maybe you sense hard work or being attuned to nature? Maybe you see someone trying to do something impossible, even though that's a little different from the traditional meaning. Read it the way that makes sense to you!

The beginning of your deck consists of 22 cards called the Major Arcana. We'll talk later about the difference between the Major and Minor Arcana in tarot. Meanwhile, let's start the journey with the Fool.

0 THE FOOL

keywords: journey, new beginnings, leap of faith

Looking at the card, you can see that the Fool is a traveler. Though the name sounds like an insult, it's actually just a description: The fool doesn't know anything yet. That makes him or her hopeful and enthusiastic. The Fool is starting a journey and is full of innocence, optimism, and energy.

I THE MAGICIAN

keywords: mastery, invention, power

The Magician is a fun card to get—it suggests someone who is in his or her own element and is starting projects and getting things done. The Magician seems to make things appear out of the air. You know that friend of yours who seems to do magical things and is never flustered? That's what the Magician represents.

II THE HIGH PRIESTESS

keywords: intuition, magic, secret, power

She is mysterious and magnetic, and she knows exactly what she's doing. The High Priestess tells you to trust your intuition and to look to your dreams for answers. She calls on you to look at what is underneath a situation and to summon your inner strength. Her message to you: There are deeper things happening, so trust your gut.

III THE EMPRESS

keywords: motherly love, beauty, support

The Empress tells you that everything is going to be fine—you'll be supported in whatever you do. She suggests abundance and beauty. She's a great card to get if you're creative and looking for encouragement for your next project. It could mean you tend to mother other people, but it doesn't suggest that's a bad thing. The card could also refer to a mother figure in your life.

IV THE EMPEROR

keywords: authority, tradition, security

The Emperor brings with him conformity and status, and a love of the way things are. But with that comes security and stability, and great structure in which to flourish. He can be stifling and isn't big on the emotions, though, so a little of this energy goes a long way! This card could also refer to a father figure in your life.

V THE HIEROPHANT

keywords: spirituality/the church, dogma, traditional values

When the Hierophant visits you in a reading, he brings dogma and creed with him. The Hierophant can represent traditional religious values and other institutions. He also offers energies of wisdom and philosophy and an invitation to work on your own spirituality. The Hierophant card can also be about teaching or learning.

VI THE LOVERS

keywords: relationships, a choice, harmony

You might think a card called the Lovers has to do with love—and you'd be right! But the Lovers is more than that. This card can mean harmonious relationships, great partnerships, and true love. It can also mean you're facing a decision about which you have to make an important choice.

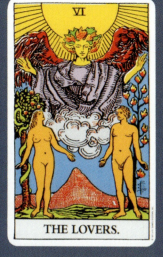

VII THE CHARIOT

keywords: success, control, willpower

When the Chariot rides into your reading, you are looking at success and victory! In the Lovers card, you made a choice and now you are running down your path at breakneck speed—maybe even literally going on a trip. The Chariot is kept in control by sheer willpower, so keep your focus and concentration, and you'll be successful!

VIII STRENGTH

keywords: courage, patience, vitality

The Strength card brings with it—you guessed it— strength! This is a card about strength under fire and sticking to your values no matter what. This card calls you to tame your lesser instincts and to use them to better a situation. Have patience and compassion, this card says, and you can make a situation turn out OK.

IX THE HERMIT

keywords: solitude, withdrawal, self-reflection

This is a card of turning inward—the Hermit asks you to take time out from the hubbub of everyday life and take a look at yourself. Contemplate what you are doing and whether it aligns with who you are or who you want to be. The Hermit tells you to withdraw for a little while and find yourself.

X THE WHEEL OF FORTUNE

keywords: good luck, change, cycles

This is the card of good luck, but also of "what goes around, comes around." If you've been having a hard time lately, this card tells you things will look up soon! The Wheel of Fortune tells you a change is coming. Depending on where it is in the reading, it's probably going to make things brighter!

XI JUSTICE

keywords: fairness, truth, ruling

Justice tells you that a fair outcome will happen, provided you have done your part. There are consequences to your actions, but the result will be fair and balanced. This card could refer to a real-life situation with a judge. It can also call on you to look at all sides and to take into account all the information of a situation.

22 MAJOR ARCANA

0 Fool   21 More Trumps

56 MINOR ARCANA

4 suits of 14 cards each = 56

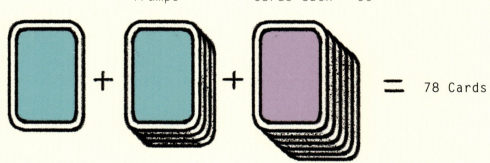

= 78 Cards

MINOR ARCANA

King   Queen   Knight   Page   Ace

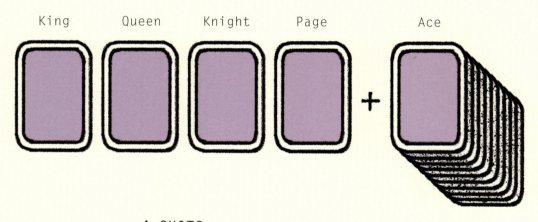

4 SUITS

Wands   Cups   Swords   Pentacles

MAJOR VS. MINOR ARCANA

THE TAROT IS DIVIDED INTO TWO SECTIONS.

The Major Arcana, or "trump cards," are considered to be the most important.

The Minor Arcana cards deal with the more day-to-day energies in a reading.

The tarot is divided into two sections. The major arcana refer to bigger life moments and to the big energies that thread through your readings.

When you look at the Major Arcana cards in order of their numbers, you'll see that they follow close to a life's journey. The Fool (number 0 in the cards) represents a person starting on the journey of life—full of hope, promise, and naiveté. By the end of the Major Arcana—number 21, The World—the Fool has been through a lot and is changed.

But at the end, he has gained the whole world and the wisdom that follows. Major Arcana cards in a reading signify big things.

Though important, the Minor Arcana cards don't represent huge change or upheaval. They are great for looking at the smaller ways you can change a situation, as well as how to change your attitude.

Together with the Major Arcana, the tarot is an amazing, complex system that can give you the insights you are searching for!

XII THE HANGED MAN

keywords: time out, incubation, perspective

A card with the term "hanged man" on it seems scary, but really this card is asking you to look at things from a different perspective. You might be at a crossroads and need to think a little more. Take time out from a situation and meditate on it for a while. Have you looked at it from all sides? The Hanged Man can mean delays and frustration, but he calls on you to tap into your inner reserves of patience.

XIII DEATH

keywords: transformation, new beginning and endings, change

Movies love to show people turning over the Death card to signify danger—but in reality, the Death card is about transformation and new beginnings. This card tells you that something in your life that isn't serving you should go away. The Death card asks you to end what isn't working and to begin something new.

XIV TEMPERANCE

keywords: equanimity, balance, serenity

When Temperance shows up in your reading, she's asking you to be calm, to look at a situation with grace and patience, to seek peace and harmony in whatever is happening, and to tap into some self-control. This is the card of moderation—find those places in your life that seem unbalanced and look for ways to ease up.

XV THE DEVIL

keywords: addiction, obsession, trapped

The Devil seems to be a scary card, but it comes with a message: If you feel trapped, you have the means to get out. This card indicates an obsessive personality, negativity, a destructive relationship, or addiction, and indicates that someone in a reading is neglecting his or her spiritual side. The message is: Escape what holds you back. You can do it!

XVI THE TOWER

keywords: sudden change, turmoil, collapse

On first sight the Tower seems like a horrible card to get. And it's true—it's not a card of peace and harmony. The Tower suggests a sudden change in circumstances: unexpected and in most cases unwelcome. But with this collapse comes cleansing; you can now build things up with a stronger foundation. Take heart—there is healing in a new start!

XVII THE STAR

keywords: hope, optimism, improvement

From the catastrophe of the Tower comes the hope and renewal of the Star. You have the means to attain your dreams! This is one of the best cards to get—it suggests that a previous, perhaps difficult, situation is easing up and things are going to be just fine. This is a card of hope and optimism, of beauty and faith. When the Star appears, take a deep breath: All will be well.

XVIII THE MOON

keywords: dreams, intuition, illusion

The Moon is about hidden things—it is the card of your subconscious and your dreams. The Moon asks you to check your intuition and listen to the pull of hidden tides. It also warns you to make sure your thoughts and anxieties are grounded in reality rather than in illusion and untruths.

XIX THE SUN

keywords: achievement, happiness, growth

When the Sun comes out, everything is better! This is one of the happiest cards in the deck and it tells you that whatever your endeavor is, it will be a success—especially if it's a creative one. This is the card of fulfillment, good health, achievement, and improvement. The Sun card shines on every other card in the deck, easing less positive ones and enhancing the more positive cards.

XX JUDGMENT

keywords: enlightenment, rebirth, fame

The Judgment card tells you that it's time for a rebirth. Now that you've been through the hardest things and come out the other side, you are ready to be who you are meant to be. This card suggests enlightenment, learning, growth, and in some cases, fame! You are ready to follow your calling and to engage in the world.

XXI THE WORLD

keywords: triumph, successful completion, joyful closure

The World is what it's all about—this card tells you that you've been on a long journey and it was all worth it. You are successful, happy, wise, and fulfilled. All the hard work has paid off and now what's left is to bask in your success and newfound wisdom. It's the end of an era in the best way possible.

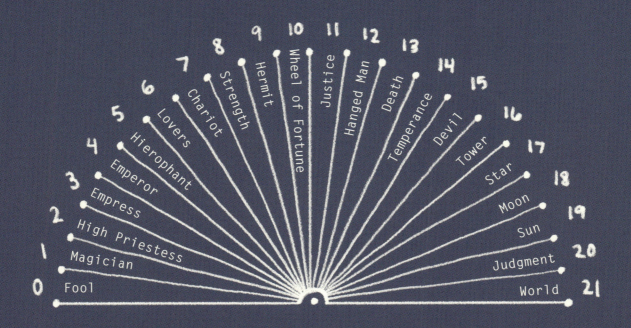

Now that you've traveled through the whole of the Major Arcana, you can see the richness and depth of the tarot! But there's more—hang on for the Minor Arcana.

CHAPTER 5

WHAT THE CARDS MEAN, PART 2: DIGGING INTO THE MINOR ARCANA

Onward to the Minor Arcana! These are the 56 remaining cards that make up the rest of the tarot deck. And they have a lot to say. Because we don't have room to tell you everything, let's focus on ways to read the cards according to their numbers and their suits. From there, you can figure out the meaning of a Minor Arcana card. Be sure to pull out a card every day—very soon, you'll know the entire deck!

Also, be sure to check out the additional resources in the back of the book. Many websites, books, and even podcasts are dedicated to the meanings of the Minor Arcana. But for now, looking at the different elements of the cards and knowing what they mean will help you get to know them as you're starting out and learning!

The first way to find the meaning of a card is to look at its suit. The tarot has four suits: swords, pentacles, cups, and wands. Each of these suits corresponds to an element and takes on characteristics of that element.

HERE ARE THE GENERAL MEANINGS OF THE SUITS AND THEIR ELEMENTS:

SWORDS. AIR. △

Air is the element of mental swiftness and quick wit. The sword suit, then, indicates clear intellect, decisiveness, and truth.

PENTACLES. EARTH. ▽

Earth is the element of work, being grounded, the material world, and finances. Pentacles suggest hard work and security, and taking a practical approach to moving through the world.

CUPS. WATER. ▽

Water is the element of relationships and deep emotion. Cups explore love and friendships—any deep feelings, really—and suggest intuition and gut feelings.

WANDS. FIRE. △

Fire is about moving fast and making things happen. Wands indicate creativity and motion, careers and physical energy, and suggest inspiration and swift movement.

After looking at the suit of the card, you can look at its number. Like a pack of playing cards, the Minor Arcana suits consist of cards numbered 1-10. These numbers have general meanings, and you can combine the number with the suit of the card to get a good sense of the card's meaning.

HERE ARE THEIR MEANINGS:

I ONES
beginnings and initiations; the purity of the suit and its best qualities

II TWOS
balancing, partnerships, seeing two sides to things

III THREES
the flowering of the suit; growth, branching out

IV FOURS
boundaries, structure, stability and settling, or doubts and restriction

V FIVES
hardships and conflict, uneven footing, challenges

VI SIXES
peace and harmony; improvement and teamwork

VII SEVENS
intention and movement, assessing a situation, dreams or illusions

VIII EIGHTS
progression and accomplishment; mastery

IX NINES
fulfillment and intensity; the full potential of the suit achieved, action and courage, self-confidence

X TENS
completion, endings and new beginnings; natural ending of the suit energy

THE COURT CARDS

You'll notice that the suits don't stop at 10—each suit has what's called "court cards," similar to the jack, queen, and king in a playing card deck. The court cards consist of pages, knights, queens, and kings.

Court cards in tarot readings can refer to a few different things. Some read the court cards as referring to a specific person—that could mean you, your friend who asked the question, or any specific person that is in the situation you're asking about. The gender of the court card doesn't necessarily have to match the person it might be referring to. Remember that tarot is about energies and types, so try not to focus on gender alone.

Others read court cards as bigger energies in a reading. So, for instance, if you get the Page of Wands in a reading, you'd read that as enthusiasm for a new project, or starting something new and creative and being willing to learn. With a court card, the energy of a card is magnified.

How you read court cards is up to you—look at the other cards in the reading and listen to your gut (and the person in front of you if you're reading for someone else).

HERE ARE SOME GENERAL MEANINGS FOR THE COURT CARDS:

PAGES
an enthusiastic newbie just beginning their path

KNIGHTS
a go-getting, intense person getting things done, but maybe going to extremes

QUEENS
an experienced person with a feminine energy; she leads by example and inhabits the inner qualities of a suit

KINGS
a masculine energy that often reads as paternal; they hold a lot of responsibility and they are a solid and stable expression of their suit

The Minor Arcana can give a richness and depth to your reading, and can help you look at the day-to-day energies in a spread. Together with the Major Arcana, you have an amazing tool for insight and assistance!

OTHER THINGS TO LOOK AT IN THE MINOR ARCANA:

You know that you can look at the suit and the numbers of the Minor Arcana cards to extrapolate a meaning. But there are other visual cues that can help! *Look at the colors of the card—are they bright or muted? Does one color stick out?* Look at the expressions and body language of the people. *Do they look anxious or happy? Which way are they facing?* Looking at these cards and seeing what's happening in the scene can give you a great idea of what the card it about! Above all, trust your intuition. How do you FEEL when you look at the card? That will give you a great sense of what the cards are trying to say and can help you read for yourself and others.

CLEANSING YOUR DECK

Tarot is all about energy—your energy, the person's energy you are reading for, and the general energy around you during a reading. Your cards also have their own energy. You want to make sure that when you get your deck, you infuse it with YOUR specific energy. The first thing you'll want to do is cleanse your deck. That is, you'll want to get rid of any other energies in your deck from the factory it was made in or the trip it took to the store.

This is super easy to do: When the moon is full, put your deck out to bathe in its light. The moon cleanses the deck and lets you add only the energies you want. You could add a quartz crystal on top of the deck to increase the energy from the moon. After a full night of moon bathing, you have a clean deck! Now take care to hold the deck and to spend time looking at it. This insures that your energy is part of the deck and it becomes an extension of you.

CHAPTER 6

MAKE IT YOUR OWN!

Reading tarot for yourself and your friends is one of the most fun, exciting things you can do. You've read through this book and you've drawn a card daily and you're ready to go. You will have no problem finding some willing friends to help you practice your reading!

Start with some of your closest friends and ask them if they want a reading. When they say yes, you can follow these steps at first before you make it your own.

Ask your friend if they have a specific question they want to ask. You can start with the yes/no spread, but better practice is a more complicated question, like: What will this school year look like? Or, how can I get ready to start dating? Tell your friend they can keep this question to themselves, or tell you—but that it's easier for you to read if you hear what the question is.

 Think of what spread will best fit the question. Or, make up your own! Make sure to choose (and to think about your choice) whether or not you will read a card as reversed.

 Shuffle the cards and think of your friend's question.

 Ask your friend to shuffle the cards, thinking of their question.

 Lay out the cards in your spread and look for patterns. Are there a lot of Major Arcana cards? A lot of swords? What kind of energy is in the reading, big picture-wise?

 Now read the cards for your friend and be sure to listen to what they have to say. Trust your intuition and read the way that feels the best!

These are the very basic steps in a reading, so be sure to make it your own. In fact, keep a notebook and take notes about what worked and what didn't during the reading. Ask for your friend's opinion and write that down. You could choose to always light a candle or to put down a cloth to read. Or maybe you want your friend to cut the deck after it's been shuffled. Perhaps you want to take five deep breaths before you lay out the cards. Find the rituals that feel good to YOU and allow you to be the best reader you can be!

PARTY!

With a cool new skill like tarot card reading, it's time to have a party, right? Here are some ideas to have your very own themed tarot party. Naturally, you're going to want to do some readings at your party to show off your new talent. But you can also make the whole night a tarot-stravaganza!

FOOD

Put out food trays with vegetables and rolled-up cheese. Add some tiny sword toothpicks so guests can pick them up. For cups, you can use—you guessed it!—cups, but you can also throw some chocolate coins in them to represent pentacles. For wands, get pretzel rods, dip them in chocolate, and then roll them in hot tamales. Now you have the four suits of the Minor Arcana! You can throw some MOON pies on the table and make some raspberry FOOL to nod to the Major Arcana too. What are some other foods you can think of to showcase the cards?

DECORATIONS

Of course you can dress up your room to look like your favorite card. But you can also enlist your friends in the fun. You could make props from cardboard that look like things in some of the cards. Then you could take photos reenacting the scenes! For instance, if you love the Three of Cups card, you can make cardboard or foam cups. Make some headbands full of flowers. Then you and two friends can enact what's happening in the card. You're a living tarot card!

This book is a great first step in taking your own journey through the tarot. Once you've looked through all there is here, continue your journey by checking out the additional resources and going more in-depth to discover all that the tarot has to offer. Remember that YOU get to choose your own journey—and like the Fool in the Major Arcana, take your first steps with enthusiasm, wonder, and the sense that the world will be yours!

ABOUT THE AUTHOR

Megan Atwood is an author and creative writing professor in South New Jersey. She loves spending time reading people's palms, calculating their numerology, understanding their astrology, and reading their tarot cards. When she is not writing or teaching, Megan is playing with her cats and dreaming up new ways to learn about the psychic arts.

ABOUT THE ILLUSTRATOR

Rachel Tesch is a graphic designer from Waconia, Minnesota. She found a love for book design while exploring typography and found photos in art school. When she is not working, she is watching Hulu, researching unexplained phenomena, and crushing her friends at Nintendo games.

TAROT GLOSSARY

arcana—this stands for "mysteries" or "secret"; the Major Arcana means the "Great Secret" and the Minor Arcana means the "Lesser Secret."

divination—the act of telling the future

dogma—an authoritative, traditional opinion; in the Hierophant's case, associated with the church and religious beliefs

esoteric—rare knowledge or knowledge that only a small group of people knows

psyche—the mind and personality of a person; sometimes also includes the soul

versatile—the ability to be flexible in your knowledge: to know or do many different things

ADDITIONAL RESOURCES

BOOKS

Have your parents or guardians check out these books for you!

Cynova, Melissa. *Kitchen Table Tarot.* Woodbury, MN: Llewellyn Publications, 2017.

Dean, Liz. *The Ultimate Guide to Tarot.* Beverly, MA: FairWinds Press, 2015.

Esselmont, Brigit. *Everyday Tarot.* New York: Running Press, 2018.

Hayetz, Meg. *Tarot for Beginners.* Althea Press, 2018.

Main, Sami. *How to Deal: Tarot for Everyday Life.* New York: HarperCollins, 2018.

INTERNET SITES

Use FactHound to find Internet sites related to this book.

Visit *www.facthound.com*

Just type in 9780756561017 and go.

INDEX

beginning steps, 44

Celtic Cross spread, 19
Chariot card, 28
cleansing, 42
colors, 11, 41
court cards, 40–41
cups suit, 38

Death card, 32, 35
decks, 7, 9, 10, 11
Devil card, 33

Emperor card, 27
Empress card, 27

Fool card, 26, 31
friend spread, 21

Hanged Man card, 32
Hierophant card, 27
Hermit card, 29
High Priestess card, 26
history, 9–11

inner guidance, 6

Judgment card, 34
Justice card, 29

King cards, 40, 41
Knight cards, 40, 41

Lovers card, 28

Magician card, 25, 26
Major Arcana, 7, 10, 25–29, 31, 32–35, 40, 45, 46
Minor Arcana, 7, 31, 37–41
Moon card, 34

number cards, 39

one-card spread, 17

Page cards, 40, 41
party, 45
pentacles suit, 38
personalized spreads, 23

Queen cards, 41

reversals, 22
Rider-Waite deck, 7, 9, 11

scenes, 11, 41, 45
school spread, 21
shuffling, 16
Star card, 22, 33
Strength card, 28
Sun card, 34
sword suit, 38

Temperance card, 32
three-card spread, 17
Tower card, 33

wands suit, 38
Wheel of Fortune card, 29
World card, 31, 35